Printed and published in
Great Britain by
D.C. Thomson & Co.Ltd.,
185 Fleet Street,
London EC4A 2HS.
© DC THOMSON
& CO.,LTD., 2009
ISBN 978-1-84535-382-7

This Book
Belongs To
Skyler

The bank's just been robbed! Can Bananaman catch the thief or will he escape with all the loot? Play as Bananaman or the robber and race your mate across the board to find out who'll come out on top! First one to roll a 6 starts!

PART 1

JAK'S DIY PUNK KIT!

CRIME!

Does your nasty neighbour keep nicking your balls when they go over the fence? Get revenge by leaving loads of breadcrumbs all over his car. Birds will flock to it and after they've filled their bellies they'll do a poo – all over his car!

Dad mugging you off?
Mate getting on your nerves?
Get ready to get your own back and punk 'em! Use stuff round the house to prank them good!

PAYOFF!

CRIME!

Sick of your Teacher giving you homework? Freak 'em out with this sneaky prank! Soak a hankie with milk and run round pretending you stuck your pen in your eye. When Teach comes for a look, squeeze the hanky next to your eye and the milk will squirt everywhere!

Does your Dad keep sneaking into your room to pinch your Dandy? Get sellotape and stick it from the top of your door to the bottom, all the way across. Close the door and wait. When he opens the door, he won't spot the tape and will walk right into it and get tangled up!

CRIME!

THE DANDY XTREME NEXT ISSUE

PAYOFF!

PAYOFF!

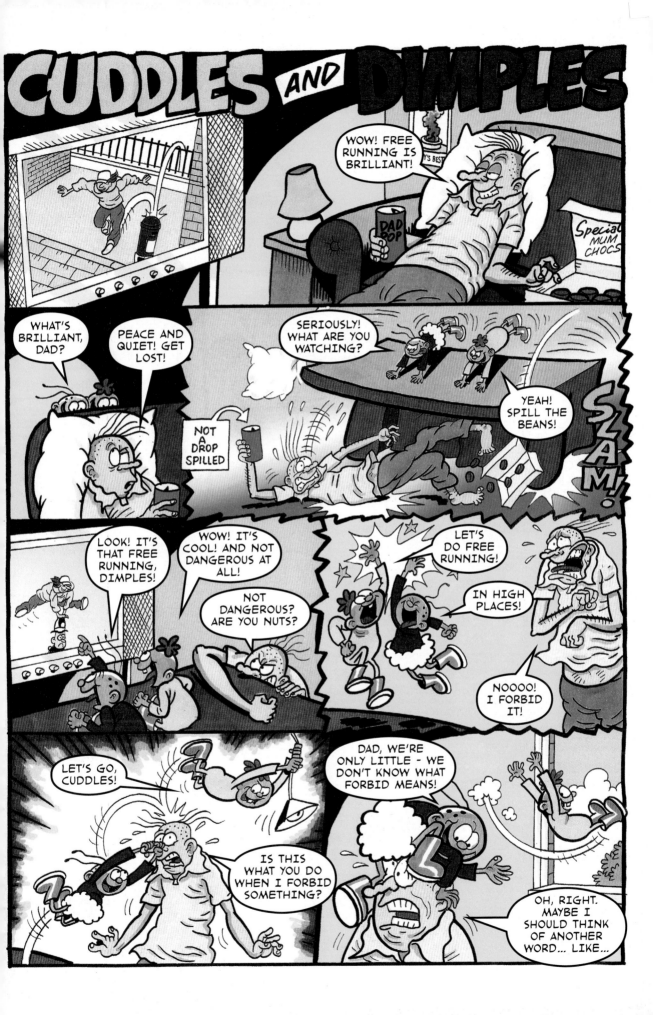

TOO PHAT

Your parents have gone out and left you with an evil babysitter! Have you got the goods to get rid of the pest or are you just a big baby? Take our awesome test and see if you can bag enough points to send that babysitter packing!

QUIT-O-METER!

For every point you bag move that babysitter along one! Remember, minus points mean you move her backwards! Will you manage to get her out the door?

It's bedtime and the babysitter from hell is trying to get you to hit the sack – what'cha gonna do?
(a) Sorted! I changed all the clocks earlier and it's already way past my bedtime! **+2**
(b) Head to bed but not to sleep – it's bed trampolining time! **+1**
(c) Ask her to tuck you in and read you a story! **0**

Uh-oh! Babysitter at one o'clock, coming to make you have a bath! How are you going to get out of it?
(a) Flush the plug down the loo! **+3**
(b) Stink her out by blasting off bubbles in the bath! **+1**
(c) Get out of it? Why? **0**

TO BE BABYSAT?

The stupid babysitter has dished up dinner but is trying to feed you and making choo-choo train noises! Tell me you've got a plan?!?
(a) Splat mash potato at her till she shuts up! **+1**
(b) Say you like plane noises better! **-1**
(c) Tell her if it goes in like a train, it comes back out like a rocket! **+5**

It's war! The babysitter is hogging the remote and making you watch Songs of Praise instead of Ben 10! Any ideas?
a) Tie her up and nab that remote! **+3**
b) Pretend your pet tarantula has escaped – she'll run for her life! **+2**
c) Sing along! **0**

The spotty teenager from across the road is babysitting you and she's HORRIBLE! You need to get rid of her – but how?
(a) Make loads of long distance calls and blame them on her! +1
(b) Draw a moustache on her in permanent marker! +4
(c) Suck up to her – she's boss! -2

You've finished your homework but the little-miss-goody-two-shoes babysitter wants you to do EXTRA! What'cha gonna do?
(a) Hide your Dandy inside a boring history book and pretend to read it! **+1**
(b) Do loads of work so she'll give you a gold star – woo hoo! **-3**
(c) Ask her to help with a science project (a wormery) and chase her out the house with the slimy worms! **+2**

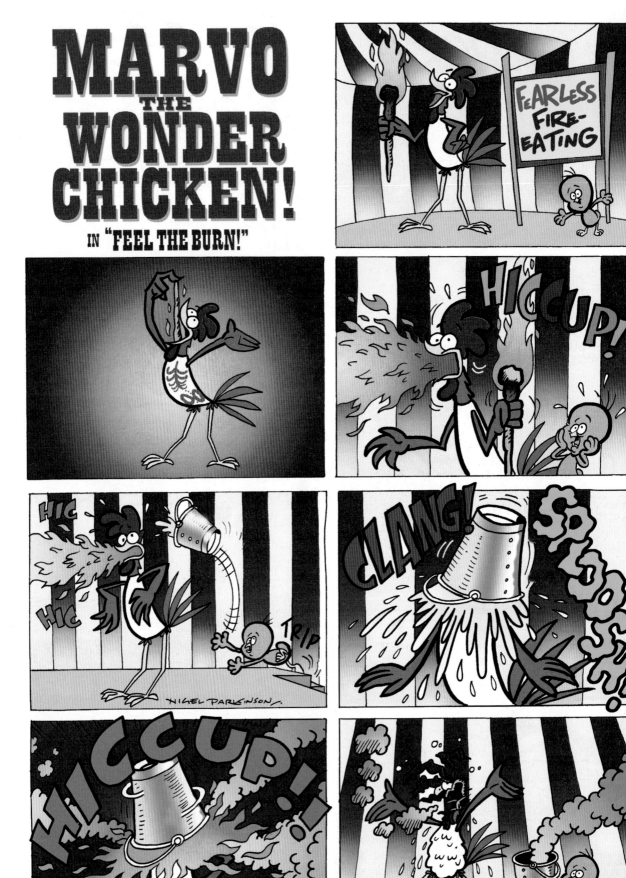

LOONY LIMERICKS

Here are some crazy poems called Limericks. Read them and try writing some of your own!

There was a young man
called Mike
Who went to the park
on his bike.
He slipped on some cake,
Fell into the lake,
Then was bit on the bum
by a pike!

There once was a
bear at the zoo,
Who always had something to do
When it bored him, you know,
to go to and fro,
he reversed it and
went fro and to.

There was a young girl called Mary,
Who wanted to become a fairy.
She tried out a spell,
Which didn't go well,
And now her hands are quite hairy.

There once was a lady named Perkins,
Who simply doted on Gherkins.
She scoffed several jars
Over twenty-four hours,
And pickled her internal workin's!

There was a young fellow from Leeds
Who swallowed six packets of seeds.
In a month, silly ass,
He was covered with grass,
And he couldn't sit down for the weeds.

There was a fat turkey named Stan,
Who went backwards wherever he ran.
He came out of the bush, Presenting his tush,
And was shot in the butt by a man.

There once was a lady
from Hyde,
Who ate a green apple
and died,
While her lover lamented,
The apple fermented,
and made cider inside
her inside.

There once was a lady named Lynn,
Who was so uncommonly thin
That when she assayed
To drink lemonade,
She slipped through the straw and fell in!

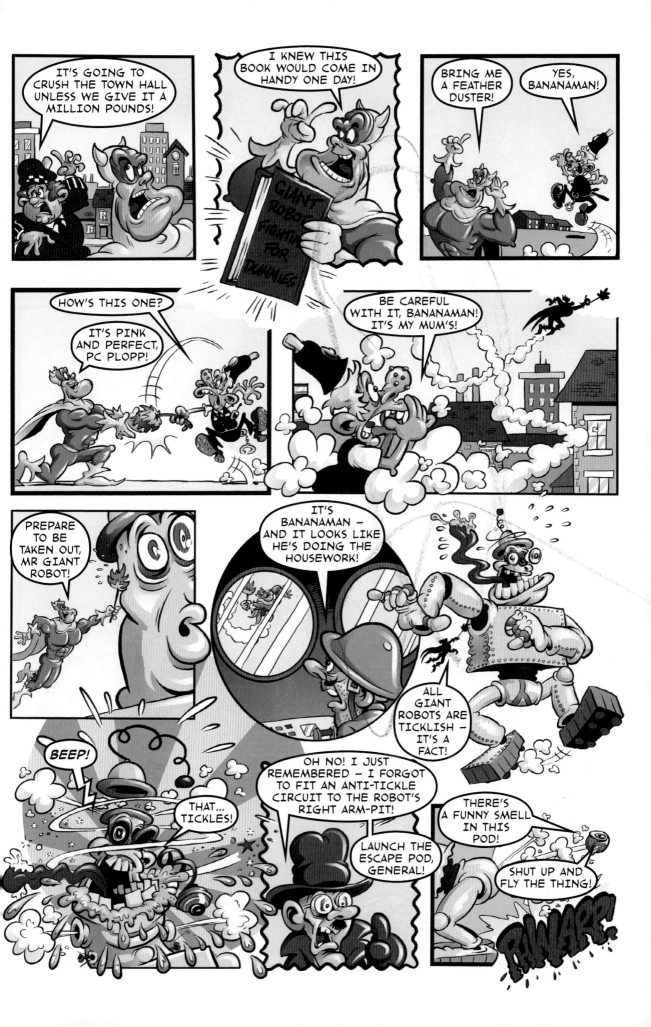

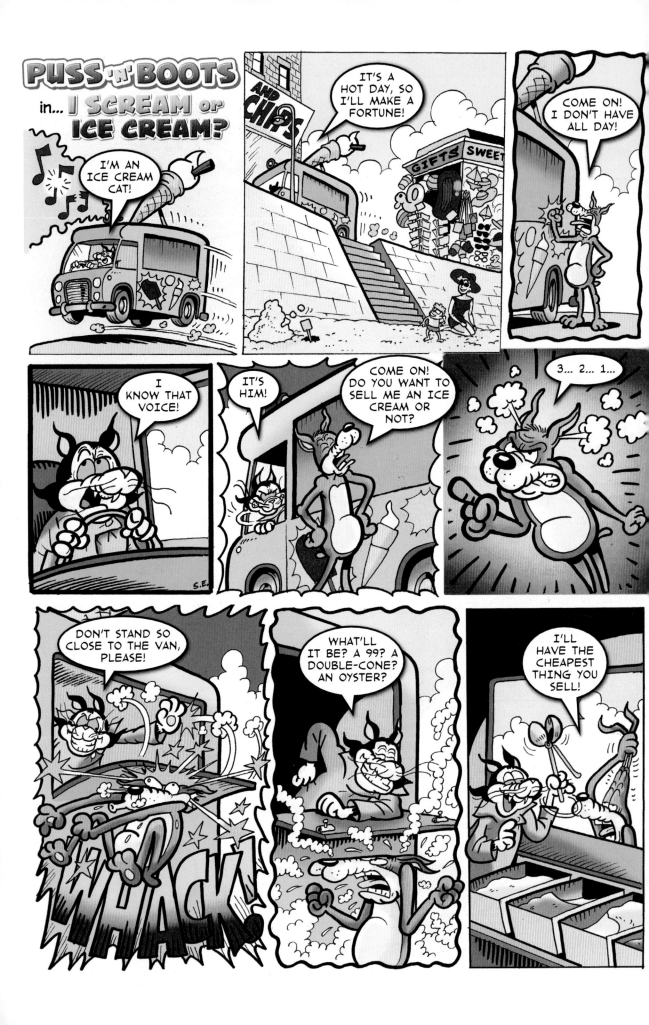

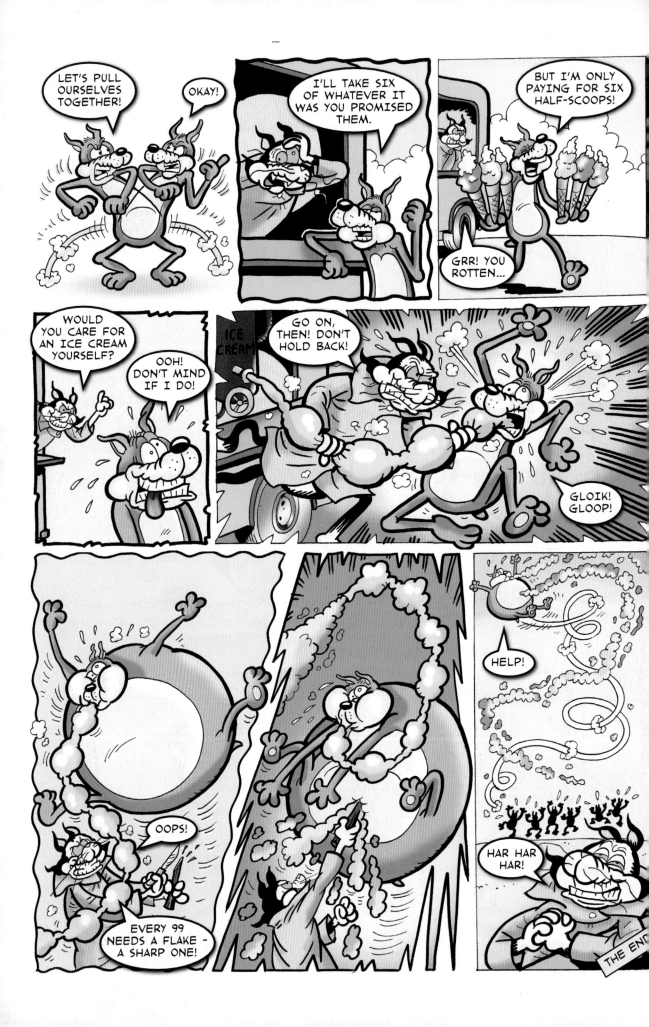

PART 2

JAK'S DIY PUNK KIT!

Is your Mum always on the phone gossiping? Stick down the handset of your house phone with blue-tak and have your mobile handy. Ring the phone and watch her try to pick it up!

CRIME!

She'll have to pull so hard, the phone will fly off and off and smack herself in the head - ouch!

PAYOFF!

Dad mugging you off? Mate getting on your nerves? Get ready to get your own back and punk 'em! Use stuff round the house to prank them good!

CRIME!

Have you got a right little smartypants in your class who thinks you're all thickos? Teach him a lesson with this prank!

1. Tell him you can balance a cup of water against the wall with just a drawing pin.

2. Go up to the wall and "accidentally" drop the pin. Ask him to grab it for you.

3. When he bends down pour the cup of water all over him – RESULT!

PAYOFF!

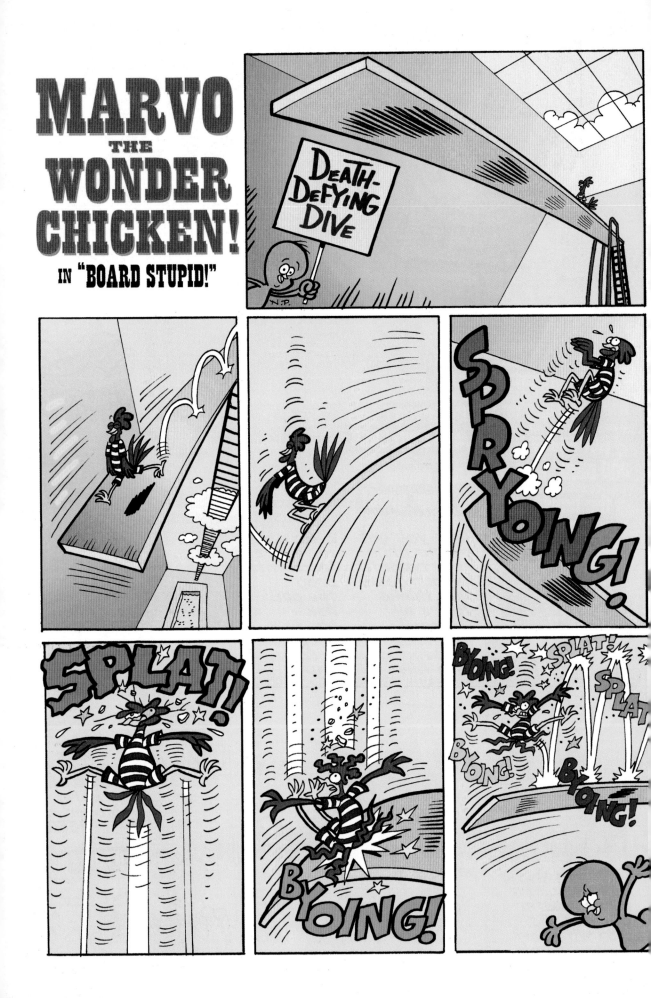

START

DESIGN-A-STUNT FOR MARVO!

Roll up! Roll up! The greatest stunt chicken on Earth is about to perform a death-defying stunt, the likes of which have never been seen before... because YOU haven't decided what he's going to do yet! Yes, it's up to you to chart the route Marvo takes through the deadly hazards you see before you (and any others you want to draw in for him)! It's CRAZY stuff, and remember – whatever happens to our intrepid wonder chicken is all your fault!

TA-DAA!

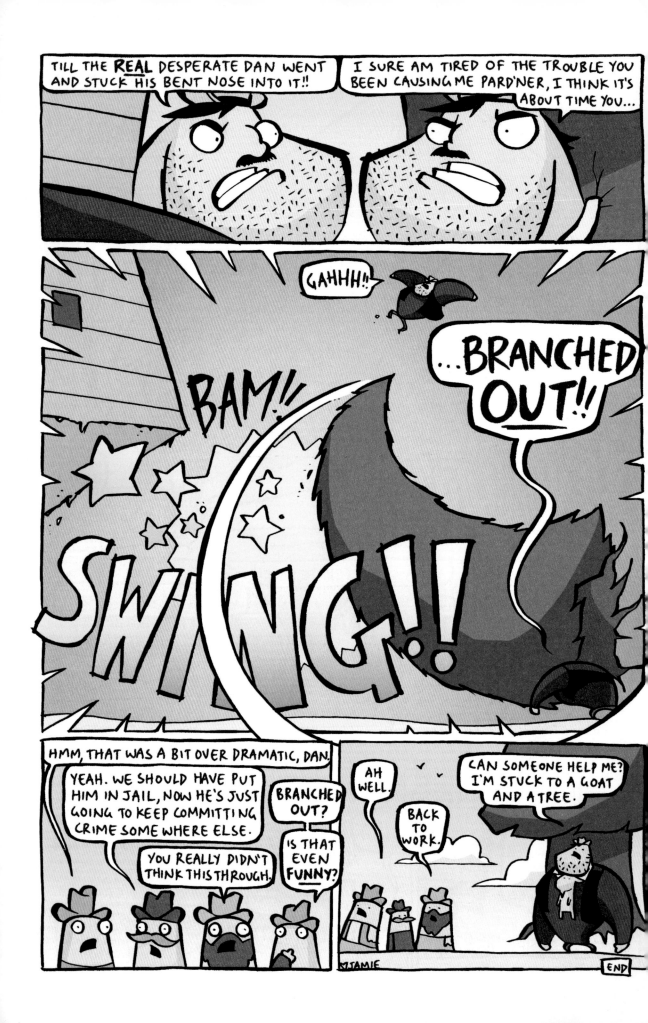

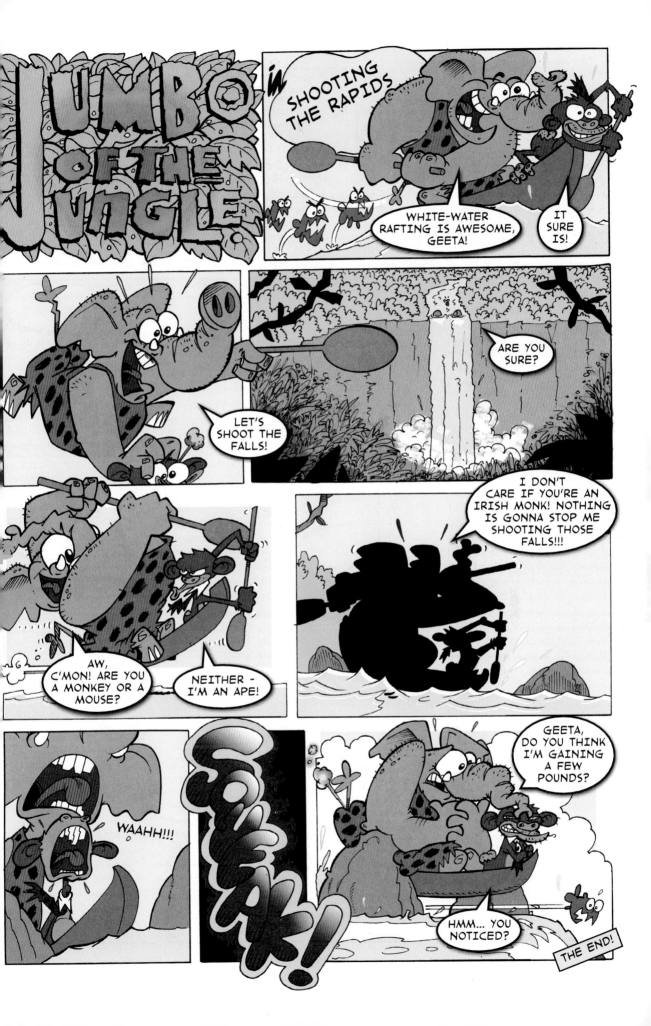

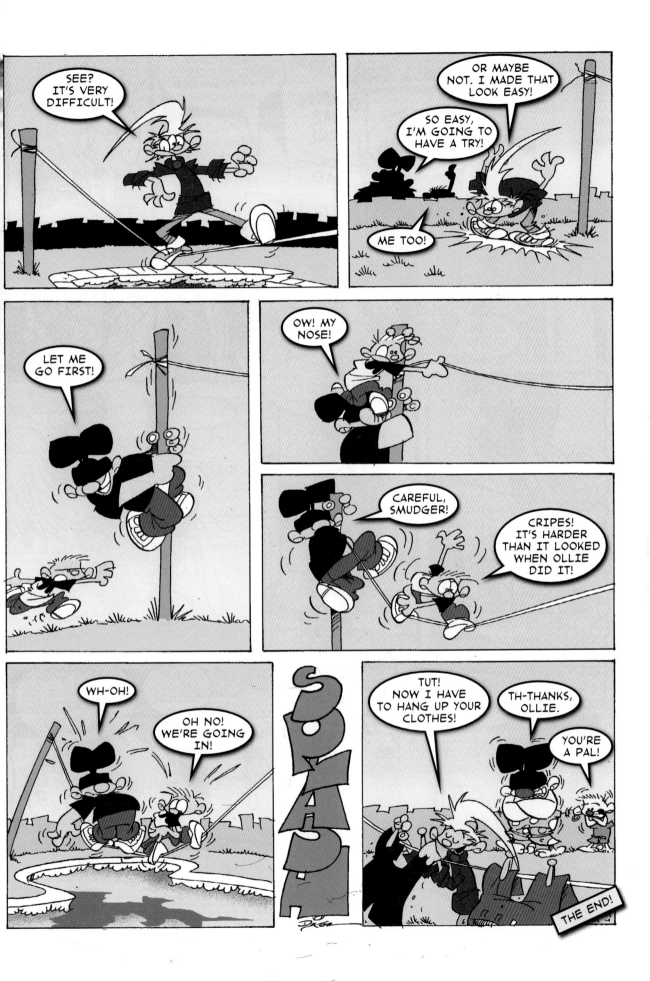

HOW TO PLAY NAPPY FAMILIES!

THE AIM IS TO COLLECT SINGLE CARDS TO MAKE UP COMPLETE FAMILIES, AND THEN TO COLLECT ALL THE FAMILIES UNTIL YOU'RE THE ONLY PLAYER WITH ANY CARDS AT ALL!

Cut out the cards, shuffle and deal them out (you can have up to four players). Work out what cards you need to complete family sets. The dealer goes first, and asks any player if he or she has a particular card i.e. Cuddles. If the player asked has the card, he must pass it to the dealer, who can then carry on asking for cards from any player. If the player asked does NOT have the card, play passes to him and he can ask for cards from any other player. Completed families should be placed face down on the table in front of the player. Once all the families are in sets, the players must collect whole families in the same way. If a player gives away all his cards, he is out – and when one player has every card, he or she is the winner! *Good luck!*

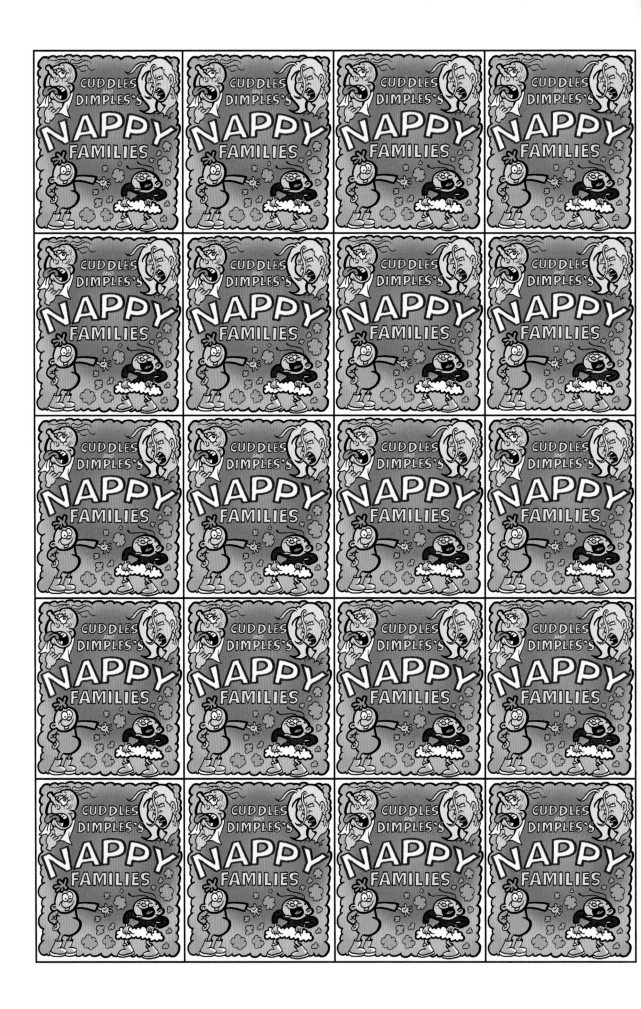

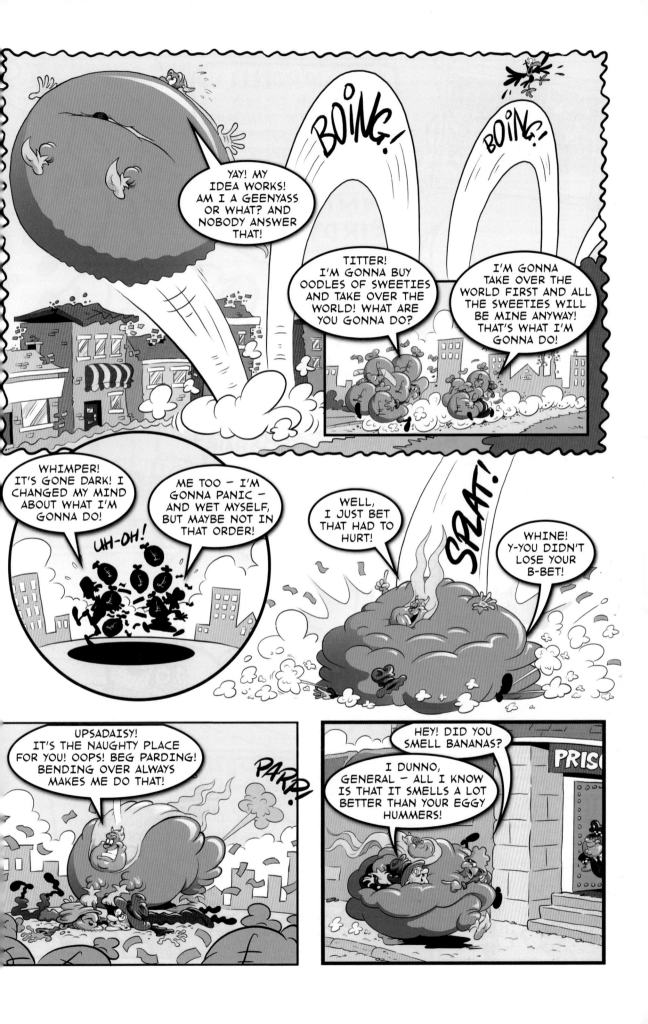

TOE-TALLY GROSS!

Yuck! Cuddles and Dimples have found their Dad's toenail clipping collection! Can you count how many grotty clippings he's stashed?

SLIMED! Cuddles and Dimples' Gran has sneezed all over this wordsearch! Now it's oozing boogers. Can you hunt out all these hidden snotty words?

bogie, snot, booger, nasal slime, nose poop, mucus, loogie, nose jam, crusty, snotter, snot ball, snail trail, bogie man, phlegm, green goblin, goober, boogerific, nose nugget, snot bubble, nose candy, snot rocket

```
X R B U V L M U C U S H E M B
L G O O B E R O P V R A C L O
S N O T B A L L X A M I S H O
N E G T E G G U N E S O N U G
O I E M I L S L A S A N O V E
S G R E E N G O B L I N T L R
E O C S N O T R O C K E T S I
P O A R I S B O G I E M A N F
O L M D A E R U I M L I G O I
O S M I R C D I E T M O R T C
P T A S N A I L T R A I L T B
Y R N A D N R T N K A L L E C
S I P R U D M G E L H P I R I
C R U S T Y M A J E S O N I L
S N O T B U B B L E R I F D A
```

BUM'S ON FIRE!

Dad's eaten too much curry and he's bursting for the loo! Can you help him find the toilet before he has an accident?

WHOSE BUTT IS THIS?

All these animals mooned Cuddles and Dimples at the zoo! Can you guess which animals were so cheek-y to the gruesome twosome?

FULL LOAD!

Mum is so mad! Cuddles has hidden loads of stuff in his stinky nappy! You've got 1 minute to sniff out what he's pinched before he's grounded for life!

YUMMY!

Someone has squished crusty old chewing gum all across this page! Can you find the hairy bits before Cuddles munches on them?

SNAP!

Cuddles and Dimples vandalised Mum and Dad's holiday photo! Can you spot their 6 changes?

BOMBS AWAY!

Cuddles thought it would be funny to feed birds baked beans! Now they're blasting off all across Dandytown! Can you work out which Dandy characters have been pooped on?

Answers: TOE-TALLY GROSS: There are 47 toenails in there; WHOSE BUTT IS THIS? (1) Pig, (2) Hippo, (3) Baboon, (4) Bear; FULL LOAD: Cuddles has stuck a remote control, banana, phone, spoon, flowers, keys, toothbrush, alarm clock, Dandy Xtreme and a rabbit in his nappy; YUMMY! There are six bits of chewing gum hidden; BOMBS AWAY! (1) Jak, (2) Bananaman, (3) Korky; SNAP! Mum has hairy armpits and a monobrow. Dad has got BillyBob teeth, socks with sandals and speedos on. Someone is mooning them and a crab has snuck on.

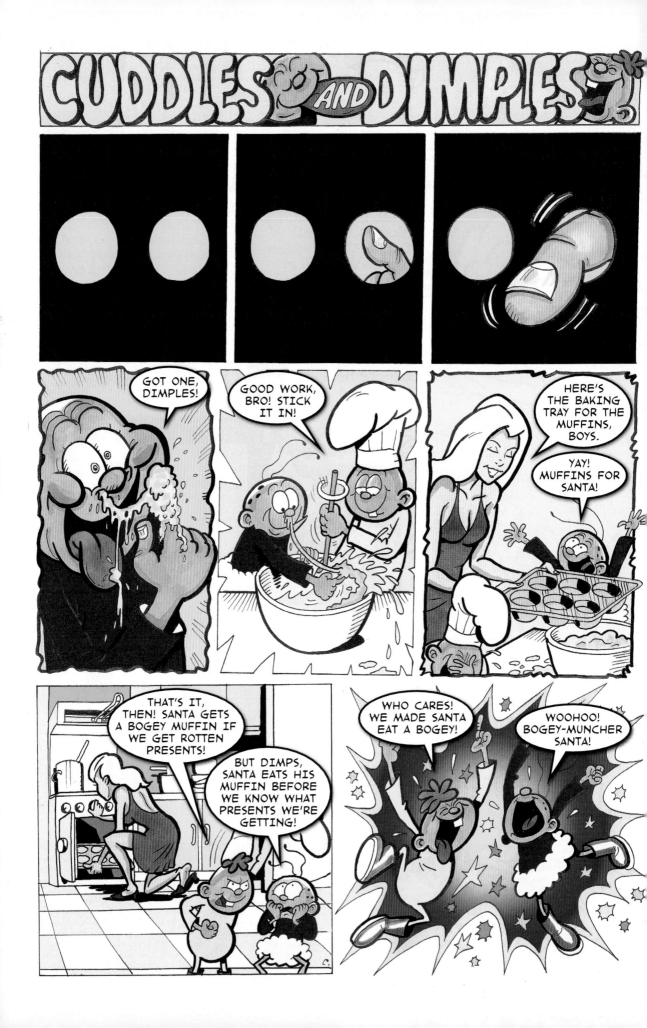

MARVO THE WONDER CHICKEN!

IN "MODEL MISBEHAVIOUR!"

PART 3

JAK'S DIY PUNK KIT!

Dad mugging you off?
Mate getting on your nerves?
Get ready to get your own back
and punk 'em! Use stuff round
the house to prank them good!

CRIME!

Is your big Sis always hogging the bathroom? Sort her out by getting a couple of sachets of tomato ketchup and sticking them to the bottom of the loo seat. When she sits her fat butt down they'll burst and cover her in sauce!

PAYOFF!

Dad's supersonic snoring keeping you up at night? Dish out some punishment by hiding loads of alarm clocks in his bedroom.

CRIME!

Is your mate always stinking the place out with his rank farts? Gross him out for a change with this revolting trick.

CRIME!

Set the first for four in the morning and then all the rest ten minutes after each other!

PAYOFF!

When he's not looking pour water into your hand, make a sneezing noise and then throw the water on the back of his neck. He'll think you've blasted snot on him!

PAYOFF!

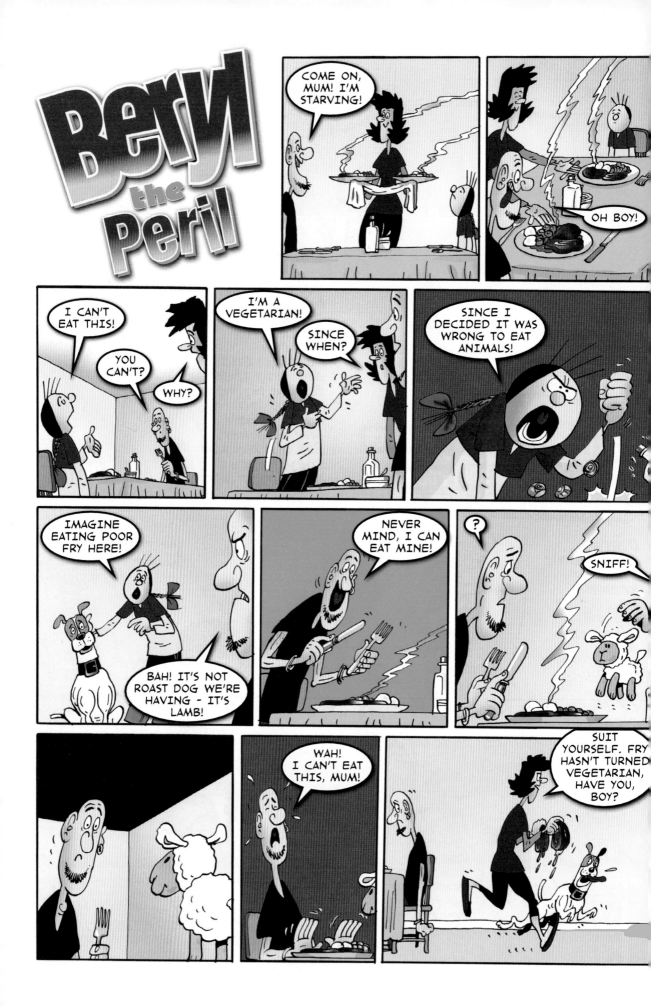

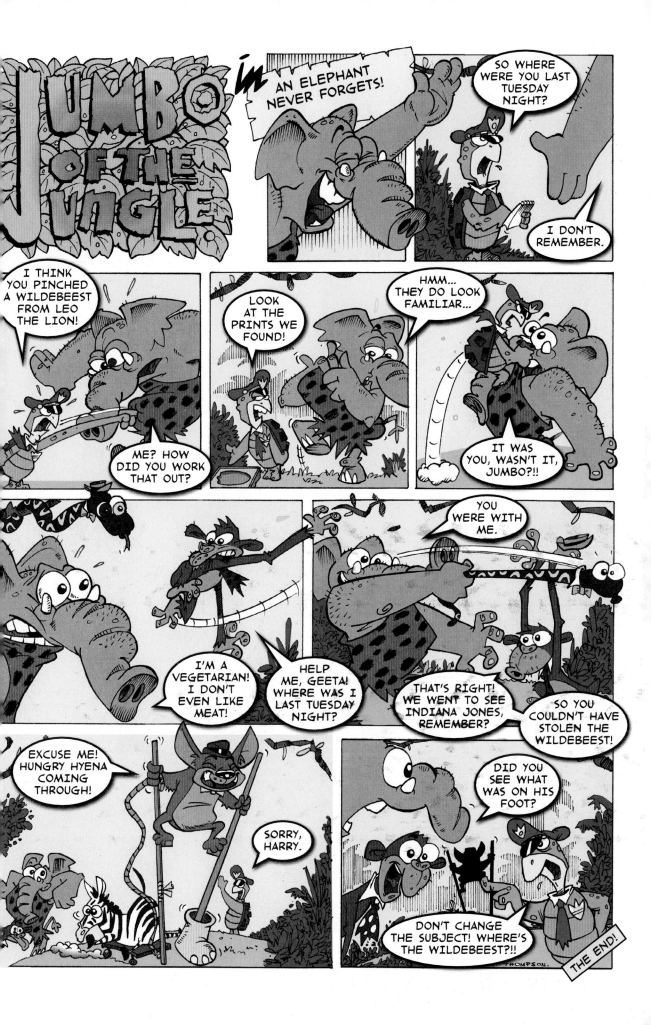

SKATEPARK SPOT THE DIFFERENCE!

There are 8 differences between these two pics of skatepark mayhem – can you find them? The solution is over the page!